Cover illustration. One of the 112 Sikorsky CH-53G medium lift helicopters of the German Army's Heersflieger taking part in the slalom event during Heli Meet International '82. Built under licence by VFW-Fokker, the last of these aircraft was delivered in 1975. (MJG)

1. Westlands have always been able to spot a project worthy of development, and the Commando assault helicopter, which is derived from the Sea King as a land-based troop transport and cargo helicopter, is no exception. The Commando Mk.1 was born in 1973 by removing the Sea King's undercarriage sponsons and making the rotor blades fixed. Further development increased its internal capacity from 17 to 28 troops, and this became the Mk.2. The Mk.2s illustrated here are from the Qatar Emiri Air Force. The type has also been sold to Egypt. (Westland Helicopters)

WARBIRDS ILLUSTRATED NO. 13

Military Helicopters

MICHAEL J. GETHING

ARMS AND ARMOUR PRESS
London—Melbourne—Harrisburg, Pa.

Introduction

Warbird 13: Military Helicopters
Published in 1983 by
Arms and Armour Press, Lionel Leventhal Limited,
2-6 Hampstead High Street, London NW3 1QQ;
4-12 Tattersalls Lane, Melbourne, Victoria 3000,
Australia;
Cameron and Kelker Streets, P.O. Box 1831,
Harrisburg, Pennsylvania 17105, USA

British Library Cataloguing in Publication Data:
Gething, Michael J.
Military helicopters. – (Warbirds illustrated; 13)
1. Military helicopters
I. Title   II. Series
623.74′ 6407   TL716
ISBN 0-85368-572-X

Layout by Anthony A. Evans.
Printed in Great Britain by William Clowes,
Beccles, Limited.

If no other proof was necessary, the South Atlantic campaign in 1982 proved to the British public that the military helicopter has a vital role in modern military operations. The American public learned that lesson during the Vietnam War. Military planners have appreciated the unique capabilities of the helicopter for at least 30 years.

The aim of this book is to illustrate the modern military helicopter, and to this end the coverage stretches back some 20 years. In that time, the tasks for which the helicopter has been used have covered the whole spectrum of air operations: liaison, communications, troop transport, casualty evacuation, assault, anti-submarine warfare, anti-surface vessel operations, search and rescue, cargo carrying, gunship duties, anti-tank warfare, and mine-sweeping. Now we see airborne early warning added to the ever-growing list.

I have attempted to ensure that every major type of helicopter from all manufacturers is illustrated within these pages. There are one or two types (notably Indian-built derivatives of the Alouette II and III) that have escaped the editorial net but, that said, I believe, a full spectrum of types and operators is provided here.

As with my previous volumes in this series, the photographs have been drawn from a wide selection of sources, including manufacturers, operators and my own collection. I would like to record specific thanks for their help to Marty Reisch of Bell, Christina Gotzheim of MBB Helicopters, Bob Carroll of Sikorsky Aircraft and Mike Farlam of Westland Helicopters. My sincere thanks are offered, albeit anonymously, to many other sources.

I would like to conclude, as I began, on a note from the Falklands conflict. It is interesting to record that on 21 May 1982 a detachment of Sea King HC.4s of 846 Naval Air Squadron lifted 912,000lb of stores and carried 520 men in that one day. Throughout the campaign, the Sea King was used at up to ten times its normal rate in atrocious weather conditions of driving rain, fog, ice and snow, at winds up to 60 knots and operating from vessels in conditions up to Sea State 7. I think the modern military helicopter is here to stay.

Michael J. Gething, Farnborough, 1983

2. This 1975 photograph shows the full line-up of Fleet Air Arm helicopters of the time: from top to bottom, a Sea King HAS.1, Wessex HAS.3, Wessex HU.5, Wessex HAR.1, Lynx HAS.2, Wasp HAS.1 and a Gazelle HT.2 – all built by Westland Helicopters. (HMS *Osprey*)

▲3 ▼4

3. Originally designed by the Sud-Est company in France, and designated SE3130, the five-seat Alouette II light helicopter was a major success both in civil and military guise. It was exported to many countries during its production lifetime (1957–1975) and was used for a variety of roles, including ASW, observation, transport, SAR (Search and Rescue) and casualty evacuation (casevac). When Sud-Est was absorbed into Aérospatiale, the Alouette II was re-designated SA313B and -C and re-fitted with the Turboméca Astazou, replacing the original Artouste I turbo-shaft. (Marine Nationale)

4. One of the five Alouette AH.2s procured as an evaluation batch for the British Army Air Corps, which led to a further procurement of twelve AH.2s. Many of these helicopters are still in service, including six deployed with United Nations forces in Cyprus. They remain a popular mount with their aircrews. (Army Air Corps Centre)

5. Following the success of the Alouette II, a slightly enlarged seven-seat version, the SE3160 Alouette III, was developed. Re-designated SA316, the Alouette III also enjoyed great export success in a wide variety of roles. This example belongs to the South African Air Force, who use it for transport, communications and light observation duties.

6. The Belgian Navy also adopted the Alouette III. This photograph, taken during Heli Meet International '82, shows the aircraft climbing away from the slalom contest, where it had been manoeuvring a bucket of water on the end of a cable around an obstacle course. Note the flotation gear forward of the main wheels. This is inflated in the event of the helicopter being forced to ditch in the sea. The Belgian Navy uses the type for SAR purposes. (MJG)

7. The French Army aviation component ALAT (Aviation Légére de l'Armée de Terre) used the Alouette III in the anti-tank role (illustrated here). Note the roof-mounted missile sight and the launchers for two SS.11 anti-tank guided missiles mounted either side of the helicopter, forward of the main wheels. (Aérospatiale)

5▲

6▲ 7▼

▲8 ▼9

▲10

11▲

8. Denmark was one of the European nations to adopt the Alouette III. This Danish Navy helicopter equipped with pontoon-type floats is demonstrating the SAR role in which it was employed. Note the rescue hoist over the crew door on the port side. (MJG)

9. The Aérospatiale SA321G Super Frelon, but without the nose-mounted radar. These aircraft are used to keep the approaches of the naval base at Brest (where the French SSBN fleet is based) clear of enemy submarines. (MJG)

10. The French Navy uses the SA321G version (illustrated) of the Aérospatiale SA321 Super Frelon for ASW work. It is equipped with search radar, dipping sonar (illustrated) and provision for four homing torpedoes. Some 24 Super Frelons of this type were built, and others have been supplied for troop transport and helicopter assault to South Africa, Israel and Libya. Others have been supplied to China in the SA321J configuration. (Aérospatiale)

11. The SA330 Puma was designed initially in 1962 for a French Army requirement. In 1967 it formed one third of the Anglo-French helicopter package along with the SA341 Gazelle and WG13 Lynx. This photograph shows an SA330B of ALAT disembarking French paratroops on exercise. (Aérospatiale)

12. An SA330E Puma HC.1 of 230 Sqn., RAF, unloading Belgian troops during Exercise 'Summer Tiger' in July 1982. The RAF has two squadrons of Pumas (Nos. 33 and 230) and in 1980 ordered a further eight Pumas to improved HC.2 standard, to supplement the original 40 HC.1 versions. (SAC P. Boardman, RAF Gutersloh)

12▼

▲13 ▼14

13. South Africa was one of several countries to order the SA330C export version, an example of which is illustrated. Powered by a pair of Turboméca Turmo IIIC turboshaft engines, the Puma can carry 16–20 troops and has provision for a variety of external stores. (Simon R. P. Thomson)

14. This photograph shows another ALAT Puma, but in updated configuration with aerials mounted on either side of the cockpit and enlarged engine air intakes with integral filters. (MJG)

15. The Aérospatiale SA341 Gazelle light observation helicopter is another of the three Anglo-French package helicopters. This photograph is unusual in that it shows a standard British Army SA341B Gazelle AH.1 sporting Australian 'Roo' roundels, as it was flown as an Australian entry during Heli Meet International '82 by an Australian Army officer seconded to the Army Air Corps. The 'Roo' roundels were removed immediately after the contest. (MJG)

16. By way of contrast, this photograph shows the latest configuration of the British Army Gazelle AH.1. It is fitted with the new Ferranti AF532 helicopter observation sight over the port crew position and, as a result of Falklands experience, an external stores pylon, here mounting a small rocket pod. (MJG)

17. Another variation on the Falklands theme is displayed by this Gazelle AH.1 of 3 Commando Brigade Air Squadron. This aircraft, shown at Army Air '82 in July 1982, was actually used in the conflict. Apart from the armament pylon, it features an upturned exhaust shroud to deflect hot gases away from the aircraft, which would otherwise serve as a heat source for an IR-seeking surface-to-air missile. Note also the internally-mounted standard Nato 7.62mm general purpose machine-gun pintle-mounted at the edge of the cockpit; and it is also just possible to see the tracks of several bullet holes, highlighted for the occasion with rods and arrow markers. (MJG)

15▲

16▲ 17▼

▲18

▲19 ▼20

18. This French ALAT SA342 Gazelle is armed with four HOT anti-tank guided missiles and a roof-mounted sight. The French Gazelles are also having their exhaust shrouds upturned to enhance their survivability over the battlefield. (MJG)
19. Egypt is one of the foreign countries that have bought the SA342 uprated version of the Gazelle. The example

21▲

shown here has a TOW anti-tank guided
missile fit. The roof-mounted sight is
developed from the one fitted to the
British Lynx helicopters. (Hughes Aircraft)
20. The SA350/355 Ecureil has been
designed as a follow-on to the Alouette II,
but it has yet to achieve the sales
success of its predecessor. This Brazilian
Navy SA350 Ecureil was manufactured
under licence by Helibras. Australia has
recently ordered the type as a training
helicopter. (Aérospatiale)
21. The SA.361H Dauphin shown here is
a military version of the civil SA360,
configured as an anti-tank helicopter,
armed with four HOT missiles on either
side of the fuselage, with a roof-mounted
sight and a nose-mounted SFIM/TRT
FLIR targeting system. (Aérospatiale)
22. The most recent Dauphin version is
the AS365F Dauphin 2, fitted with the
nose-mounted Agrion 15 search radar and
armed with four Aérospatiale AS-15TT
anti-ship missiles. The type has been
ordered by Saudi Arabia. This mock-up
was photographed when on display at the
1981 Paris Air Show. (MJG)

22▼

▲23

▲24 ▼25

26▲

23. One of the three Agusta A109s ordered by the Italian Army, configured with a nose-mounted sight and four TOW anti-tank missiles. The evaluation of this aircraft led to the decision to go-ahead with a dedicated anti-tank/scout helicopter, designated A129. (Agusta)

24. The spoils of war: this A109 of the Argentinian Army was captured by 3 Commando Brigade Air Squadron, Royal Marines, during the battle for Port Stanley on 14 June 1982. The helicopter, one of the two A109s brought back to the UK, is seen here at Middle Wallop in July 1982, and is wearing RM insignia. (MJG)

25. The Italian Carabinieri find the A109 a useful machine for policing operations with its seven-man payload plus pilot. Note the twin landing/searchlights in the nose. (MJG)

26. This model depicts the Agusta A129 Mangusta (Mongoose) two-seat anti-tank/scout helicopter. Note the stub wings housing eight TOW anti-tank missiles on the outer pylons and rocket pods on the inner ones, the sighting system in the nose and the 'crashworthy' undercarriage construction. The prototype A129, powered by two Rolls-Royce Gem turboshaft engines, is scheduled to fly in September 1983. (Agusta)

27. Agusta build several types of American-designed helicopters under licence. This Agusta-Bell AB.205 of the Greek Army corresponds to the UH-1D/H from Bell. (Agusta)

27▼

▲28

28. The AB.206B JetRanger II is another Agusta-Bell product, corresponding to the Bell 206 JetRanger (or OH-58A in US service). (Agusta)

29. One of the benefits of licence-building another company's design is that it may be re-configured to another role. Agusta have done very well with the AB.212, converting it to carry ASW equipment and radar (the Canadian Marconi AN/APN-208(V2) system) and also equipment to operate in the anti-surface vessel (ASV) role. Designated AB.212ASW, it has been sold to the navies of Italy, Peru (illustrated) and Ecuador. (Simon R. P. Thomson)

30. Sikorsky is another company with whom Agusta have a licence deal. This Agusta-Sikorsky SH-3D (Sea King) of the Peruvian Navy is armed with the AM.38 air-launched version of MM.38 Exocet, the predecessor of the AM.39 Exocet. (Agusta)

31. Three Bell AH-1G HueyCobras of the 7th Sqn., 1st Cavalry Regiment, US Army seen over the Mekong Delta in Vietnam. The aircraft, thought to be from 'A' Troop, were based at Vinh Long. (Bell)

32. Three Bell UH-1D Iroquois from the 229th Assault Helicopter Battalion, 1st Cavalry Division (Airmobile) in the unmistakeable environment of Vietnam. Note the door-mounted M60 machine-guns to provide suppressive fire support in the assault. (Bell)

▲29   ▼30

▲33 ▼34

33. One of the three latest Model 414 Chinooks delivered to the Spanish Army's air component. They will be assigned to Battalion Helicopter Transport 5, bringing the number of Chinooks in service there to twelve, all of which are based at Colmenjar, Spain. (Boeing Vertol)

34. With over 200 Black Hawks in service, the UH-60A is set to become the UH-1D of the 1980s. This photograph shows one of the first aircraft assigned to the US Army, carrying a full load of eleven combat-equipped troops plus a flight crew of three. (Sikorsky)

35. A further derivative of the SH-3D is the HH-3F, which is again part of the Agusta-Sikorsky licence deal. Some twenty of this version have been built for the Italian Air Force search and rescue (SAR) organization. The HH-3F is amphibious – a useful asset for its SAR role. (Agusta)

36. In 1967, a new consortium, Elicotteri Meridionali, was set up by the Italian aerospace industry to build the Boeing Vertol CH-47C Chinook under licence. Agusta and SIAI-Marchetti are major contributors to the programme. This is an EM CH-47C Chinook of the Italian Army, photographed during Army Air '82 at Middle Wallop. (MJG)

37. One of the first export orders received for the EM CH-47C Chinook was from the Imperial Iranian Army in the early 1970s, an example of which is illustrated here. Orders have also been received from Libya and Morocco. (Agusta)

35▲

36▲ 37▼

▲38

38. The Bell UH-1 Iroquois series was destined to become one of the most successful helicopters of the Vietnam War. The aircraft illustrated is a US Navy UH-1B version, configured for armed support, flying low over the riverine environment of Vietnam's southern coast. In this configuration, the UH-1B could carry seven troops plus two crew, and two 0.50in machine-guns on external stations either side of the fuselage. (Bell)

39. The UH-1 series was built under licence by Mitsui/Fuji in Japan. The helicopter illustrated is a Japanese Ground Self Defense Force (Army) version.

40. American infantrymen leap from a UH-1D Iroquois (soon to be dubbed the 'Huey') during the Vietnam War. The UH-1D was the major production variant of the series, powered by a Lycoming T53-L-11 turbo-shaft engine, and able to carry twelve troops plus one pilot. (Bell)

41. The 'Huey' became one of the work-horses of the Vietnam War. This UH-1D is being used in the medical evacuation (medevac) role. Note the CH-47 Chinook in the background. (Bell)

42. This UH-1H, seen here unloading Republic of Korea infantry during Exercise 'Team Spirit '80', is the -D model fitted with an uprated Lycoming T53-L-13 power plant. Note the upturned engine exhaust, designed to enhance its survivability against heat-seeking missiles. (S/Sgt Ken Bach, US Army)

▲39 ▼40

▲43

▲44 ▼45

43. The US Navy's general-purpose version of the UH-1B, fitted with T53-L-13 engines and re-designated TH-1L, signifying its new role as a trainer. (Bell)

44. As the UH-1 series developed, it was realized that there was a need for a twin-engined version. The result was the Model 212. Fitted with a Pratt and Whitney Canada PT6T-3 Turbo Twin Pac engine installation, it became the UH-1N. The example illustrated belongs to the US Marine Corps. (USMC)

45. In Canadian Forces service, the UH-1N is known as the CH-135. It can carry thirteen troops, plus crew, or six stretcher cases and one medical attendant in the medevac role. (Bell)

46. Bell's Model 214 took the UH-1 series a stage further, being designed to carry eighteen troops plus a pilot in its ultimate 214ST version. The project was instigated by Iran, and the 214ST was to have been built in that country. In the event, only the 214A models were delivered before the fall of the Shah. This photograph illustrates the 214ST prototype, which has not yet achieved military status but is now in production for the civil market. (Bell)

47. The military version of the Model 206 JetRanger is designated the OH-58 Kiowa by the US Army. It is a particularly successful helicopter on the civil as well as the military market. This photograph shows an Australian Army Kiowa. (Bell)

48. Many of the OH-58A Kiowa models in US Army service have been updated to improve their performance and survivability. An Allison T63-A-720 turbo-shaft engine has been installed and the curved windscreen has been replaced by a flat-plate canopy to reduce glint. Some 585 OH-58Cs are planned. (Bell)

46▲

47▲ 48▼

23

▲49

▲50 ▼51

52▲ 53▼

49. A further update of the Kiowa is planned by the US Army in the form of the AHIP programme (Advanced Helicopter Improvement Program). This retouched photograph shows an OH-58A brought up to AHIP standard (to be designated OH-58D). The major modifications are obvious, such as the McDonnell Douglas/Northrop mast-mounted sight and the General Dynamics Stinger self-defence missiles. (Bell)

50. Another modification of a standard civil helicopter is the TexasRanger version of the 206L LongRanger. It offers increased payload and the ability to carry anti-tank missiles and other armaments. (Bell)

51. Having proved their usefulness in the gunship role early in the Vietnam War, the UH-1 series was developed into a dedicated gunship configuration, after initial experience with the Bell 207 Sioux Scout prototype. The requirement was issued in 1964 and an order for 100 placed with Bell in 1966. The example illustrated is an AH-1G HueyCobra, as the type was designated, firing its 2.75in rockets. (Bell)

52. In 1975, a version of the AH-1G HueyCobra entered service installed with Hughes TOW (Tube-launched, Optically-tracked, Wire-guided) anti-tank missiles. This photograph shows an AH-1S (Modified) Cobra, the first in the three stages of development, fitted with eight TOW launchers, but retaining the nose turret. (UKLF)

53. The end product of AH-1S development: the AH-1S (Modernized) with the full weapons and sensor package installed, as well as the uprated T53-L-703 power plant. (Bell)

▼54 ▲55

54. A further stage in AH-1S development has been test-flown by Bell in their Model 249. Designated YAH-1S, it features the four-blade rotor developed for their Model 412 programme, and it offers significant improvements over earlier models in terms of agility and power control. (Bell)

55. The AH-1G Cobra was developed with the same engine as the UH-1N, the Pratt and Whitney Canada Turbo Twin Pac. In US Marine Corps service, the AH-1G became the AH-1J SeaCobra, 69 of which were procured from 1970. (Bell)

56. The SeaCobra received a further update when the last two AH-1Js were used as prototypes for the AH-1T. With an uprated power pack, a fuselage and tailboom stretch and the dynamic system of the Model 214, the first of 57 AH-1Ts entered USMC service in 1977. This AH-1T SeaCobra is seen on board the USS *Saipan* in 1980. (MJG)

57. In 1972, Iran ordered 202 AH-1J SeaCobras from Bell, 62 of which were TOW-capable. Since the first delivery in 1974, they have seen action in the Iran-Iraq war. (Bell)

▲58

▲59 ▼60

58. This photograph shows one of the two prototypes of the Model 409 YAH-63, which was the Bell contender for the US Army's Advanced Attack Helicopter programme. It made its first flight in October 1975. Based on the Bell Model 309 KingCobra, a company-funded development, the YAH-63 shared the same GE T-700 power plant as its rival, the YAH-64, as well as the same armament. The programme was discontinued after the Hughes entry was selected in December 1976. (Bell)

59. The shape of things to come . . . Bell's XV-15 tilt-rotor experimental craft, seen here in vertical flight, is a cross between a helicopter and a turboprop aircraft. The tilt-rotor concept is now being studied for a whole series of helicopter replacement aircraft for the 1990s under the JVX project, in which Bell has teamed up with Boeing Vertol. (Bell)

60. A UH-46D Sea Knight of the USS *Savannah*. First flown in 1958, this helicopter became the US Marine Corps' standard transport/assault helicopter, as well as serving in the SAR and vertrep (vertical replenishment) roles with the US Navy. All Sea Knights in US service are currently undergoing a Safety, Reliability and Maintainability programme to see them into the 1990s. (Boeing Vertol)

61. A pair of Kawasaki-built KV-107/II-4 troop transports of the Japanese Ground Self-Defense Force, which acquired 59 of the type. The basic model is still in production in Japan in small numbers, and Kawasaki are proposing a further-developed version for the armed forces there. Note the external fuel tanks on the fuselage sides, forward of the white sponsons.

62. The Boeing Vertol Model 107 was also supplied to Canada in 1964. Six CH-113 Labradors (similar to the CH-46A) and five CH-113A Voyageurs were supplied for SAR and troop transport respectively. Both versions are now the subject of a Search and Rescue Capability Up-grading Program (SARCUP), being fitted with extra fuel tanks, improved avionics, weather-mapping radar and an external winch. This photograph shows the first helicopter to be completed – a CH-113A Voyageur. (Boeing Vertol Canada)

63. A Marine Corps CH-46F of HM 461 on board the USS *Saipan* in 1980. In this role it can carry 25 troops or 4,000lb of cargo. It is powered by a pair of GE T58-GE-10 turbo-shaft engines. Note the weathered low-visibility camouflage and markings on this example. (MJG)

61▲

62▲ 63▼

64. An RAF Chinook HC.1 of 18 Sqn. carries a Spartan APC on its cargo hook during Exercise 'Live Log' in 1981. The arrival of the Chinook in RAF service, first mooted in 1962, finally came in 1981. The following year, the only Chinook survivor of the loss of the *Atlantic Conveyor* would give sterling service to the Task Force in the South Atlantic. (R. L. Ward)

65. A US Army CH-47C Chinook displaying its various access panels during routine maintenance prior to taking part in the 1982 Yeovilton air display. The Chinook is powered by a pair of Lycoming T55-L-11A turbo-shaft engines. It can carry 44 troops (although in the Falklands an RAF HC.1 took 81 'paras' in one hop) or 28,000lb external cargo. Note the small box on the rear fuselage by the ramp, which is a chaff/flare dispenser for self-defence. (MJG)

66. An unusual view of a CH-47C of the US Army showing troops climbing up an airborne ladder to reach the cabin during an exercise at Ft. Campbell in Kentucky. Careful observation of the underside will reveal the central cargo hook suspended from the Chinook. (UKLF)

67. One of the seven CH-147 (CH-47C) Chinooks assigned to 450 Sqn. of the Canadian Armed Forces. Canada ordered nine CH-147 Chinooks, and delivery began in 1974. They featured Avco Lycoming T55-L-11C engines, advanced flight control systems, crashworthy fuel tanks, a 28,000lb cargo hook and forward door rescue winch. (Boeing Vertol)

66▲ 67▼

▲68 ▼69

68. The first 'production' model of the improved Chinook for the US Army, the CH-47D, seen on its maiden flight on 26 February 1982. The US Army is to modernize its existing CH-47A/B/C fleet (436 helicopters in all) to CH-47D configuration. The eight improvement areas are new transmissions, redundant electrical systems, composite rotor blades, new Lycoming T55-L-712 turbo-shaft engines, modular hydraulics, triple cargo hooks, advanced flight controls and improved avionics. (Boeing Vertol)

69. The forerunner of the Hughes 500M series was the US Army's OH-6A Cayuse, which was the winner of the Light Observation Helicopter contest in 1961. One of the most compact helicopters ever built, relative to its capability, the OH-6A saw much service during the Vietnam War. The US Army bought a total of 1,434 Cayuse. This photograph shows one after being refurbished at Hughes Helicopters' Culver City facility in 1982. (Paul Beaver)

70. Despite its success in Vietnam, the Hughes 500/OH-6 Cayuse was not developed for further US Army use. The manufacturers did, however, continue development, resulting in the Hughes 500MD/TOW Defender. With a nose-mounted sight and four TOW anti-tank missiles, this small helicopter has been most successful on the export market, being sold to countries such as Israel (illustrated, during nap-of-the-earth manoeuvres) and Kenya. (Hughes Helicopters)

71. In 1980, Hughes unveiled their follow-on to the TOW Defender, the Defender II. This light attack/scout helicopter featured several new refinements, prominent among them being the mast-mounted sight, pilot's night vision system (mounted beneath the nose), an under-fuselage 30mm Chain Gun (mounted on the port side) and two General Dynamics Stinger air-to-air missiles for self-defence, which are similar to those mounted on the OH-58 AHIP helicopter. (MJG)

70▲ 71▼

▲72

▲73 ▼74

72, 73. The TOW Defender was further developed to incorporate a mast-mounted sight (MMS) in 1982. This photograph shows a TOW launch during successful firing trials. Note the changed shape of the MMS from that of the Defender II. The concept of the MMS is to allow the helicopter to mask its bulk, with the MMS being the only part of the helicopter to show itself above the skyline for observation purposes. (Hughes Helicopters)

74. At an all-up weight of 3,550lb, the Hughes 500MD/ ASW is probably the world's lightest ASW helicopter. It is equipped with search radar, AN/ASQ-81 towed magnetic anomaly detector (MAD) 'bird', 'popout' floats for emergencies and provision for two Mk.44 or Mk.46 torpedoes, plus two crew. It has been sold to the Spanish and Taiwanese Navies. (Hughes Helicopters)

75. The Aérospatiale/ Westland Gazelle has proved a most successful light helicopter and is in service worldwide. This SA341D Gazelle HT.3 of Central Flying School, RAF Shawbury, is seen here taking part in the Heli Meet International 1982. (MJG)

76. The Swedish Navy bought ten Agusta-Bell AB.206B JetRangers for use in the ASW and SAR role. Note the 'long-reach' skid undercarriage with 'popout' flotation gear, and the four depth bombs beneath the fuselage. (Agusta)

▲77 ▼78

77. One of the six Lynx HAS.2 helicopters sold to the Royal Netherlands Navy. Designated UH-14A these Lynx are operated by 7 Sqn. in the SAR role. A further eighteen were supplied for the ASW role, ten with dunking sonar (SH-14B) and eight with MAD gear (SH-14C). (MJG)

78. One of the few 'clean' British Army Lynx AH.1 helicopters. The majority of the 100-plus Lynx AH.1s being supplied will be fitted with eight TOW anti-tank missiles and a roof-mounted sight. (MJG)

79. The Hughes YAH-64 was the winner of the US Army's Advanced Attack Helicopter competition in 1976. Despite its curiously ungainly and insect-like appearance, it is most agile in the air. Powered by a pair of General Electric T700-GE-700 turboshaft engines, it has been built as a highly survivable anti-tank system on today's battlefield. This photograph shows the AH-64 Apache (as its production version is designated) during its first showing in the UK at Army Air '82. (MJG)

80. The fourth prototype YAH-64 Apache firing one of the sixteen Hellfire missiles it carries as its principal anti-tank armament. It is also armed with a 30mm Chain Gun beneath the fuselage, and can carry TOW missiles or 2.75in rocket pods as an alternative to the Hellfires. (Hughes Helicopters)

81. This head-on view makes the Apache appear even more ungainly than it is. Plainly visible are the T700 engine intakes, the two crewmen (the pilot being in the raised rear seat), the crash-resistant undercarriage, the Target Acquisition and Designation System/Pilots Night Vision System (TADS/PNVS) mounted in the nose, the gimbal-mounted 30mm Chain Gun and eight Hellfire missiles. (Hughes Helicopters)

79▲

80▲ 81▼

▲82

82. This unusual helicopter, the HH-43B Huskie, was developed by Kaman in response to a USAF requirement for a base rescue and SAR helicopter. The UH-43C version was used as a troop transport. In production from 1958 to 1965, the Huskie earned the nickname 'Flying Eggbeater' because of its unusual inter-meshing rotor blades. This photograph shows an HH-43B rescuing some flood-bound homesteaders in the United States. (USAF)

83. The H-2 Seasprite began life as a transport and SAR helicopter for the US Navy, but in the late 1960s it was re-configured for ASW work and, later still, in SH-2F configuration as the Mk.1 Light Airborne Multi-Purpose System (LAMPS). The SH-2F (illustrated) shows the shortened wheelbase, AN/ASQ-81 MAD gear, LN-66H radar, an external fuel tank and homing torpedo. (Kaman)

84. This view of the SH-2F Seasprite LAMPs Mk.1 helicopter clearly shows the fifteen sonobuoy dispensers over the homing torpedoes. The SH-2F was put back into production in 1981 and serves, and will continue to serve, on many types of smaller ships in the US Navy for some years. (Kaman)

85. The standard Soviet shipborne ASW helicopter is the Kamov Ka-25 Hormone. This photograph, taken on board the carrier *Kiev*, shows three 'Hormone-As'. Note the external 'box' beneath the fuselage, which houses wire-guided anti-submarine torpedoes or depth charges. (Tass)

86. Three more Ka-25 'Hormone-As' 'spotted' on the rear flight deck of a *Moskva*-class helicopter carrier. Apart from the 'Hormone-A' ASW variant, there is also a special electronic version, designated 'Hormone-B', designed for acquiring targets for ship-launched missiles. This variant is differentiated by its larger nose radome. (Novosti)

87. This photograph shows an improved variant of 'Hormone', codenamed 'Helix', seen on the flight deck of the new Soviet destroyer *Udaloy*. It features a larger cabin and strengthened horizontal stabilizer. (US Navy)

88. Another view of the 'Helix', now thought to be designated Ka-36, operating with *Udaloy*. It is understood to be powered by the twin Glushenkov GTD-3F turbo-shaft engines of the 'Hormone'. (US Navy)

▲85 ▼86

▲89

▲90 ▼91

89. The Bo.105 series from Messer-schmitt-Bölkow-Blohm (MBB) was the first significant helicopter to emerge from post-war Germany. Its military version as marketed by MBB is designated Bo.105M, and is powered by a pair of Allison 250-C20B turboshafts, capable of lifting 4-6 people or equivalent cargo or armament. The German Army has two versions in service: the VBH light observation and communications version (illustrated), 227 of which are entering service; and the PAH-1. Note the roof-mounted observation sight over the port crew seat. (MJG)

90. The Bo.105P armed with six HOT anti-tank missiles is the West German Army's first-generation anti-armour helicopter. A total of 212 have been delivered under the designation PAH-1. This photograph shows a PAH-1 firing a HOT missile. (MBB Helicopters)

91. This view of the PAH-1 clearly shows the six HOT launchers on a cantilevered weapons pylon, three either side. The Bo.105M has since been successfully equipped with TOW missiles for trials purposes. (Bundeswehr)

92. With a view to capturing the current vogue for mast-mounted sights, MBB showed a Bo.105M at the 1981 Paris Air Show fitted with a French SFIM Ophelia MMS. As can be seen from the camouflage finish, the aircraft was well nicknamed the 'flying giraffe'. (MJG)

93. This view shows the export version of the PAH-1 offered by MBB Helicopters, the Bo.105CB armed with eight TOW missiles and a roof-sight. The helicopter is finished in Swedish Army camouflage after a demonstration tour in that country. (MBB Helicopters)

92▲ 93▼

▲94

94. In 1977, MBB joined forces with Kawasaki of Japan to develop an eight – ten seat multi-purpose helicopter for both civil and military purposes. Designated BK.117, the first prototype flew in 1979. Production is underway for civil orders, but so far no military orders have been forthcoming. (MBB)

95. This artist's impression shows the joint MBB/Aérospatiale proposal for a second-generation anti-armour helicopter, designated PAH-2 (PanzerabwehrHubschrauber 2) by West Germany and HAC (Helicoptere Anti-Char) by France. At the moment the project is on the 'back burner' as Germany has funding difficulties on the defence budget. However, as can be seen from this impression, the PAH-2/HAC would be armed with

eight improved HOT missiles. (MBB Helicopters)

96. The first major Soviet-designed helicopter was the Mil Mi-2 'Hoplite', seen here on liaison duties with a troop of T-62 tanks. In 1964, production of the 'Hoplite' was transferred to the WSK-PZL Swidnik factory in Poland. Since then over 3,000 examples have been built in 24 versions, military and civil. (via UK MoD)

97. The Mil Mi-4 'Hound' was the next design undertaken and put into production in the Soviet Union. Not unlike the S-55 Whirlwind in configuration, the 'Hound' was the Soviet Union's first troop transport and ASW helicopter. This photograph shows four transport 'Hounds' in Southern Bohemia during Exercise 'Vltava' in September 1966. (C T K Mevald/Novosti)

▼95

96▲ 97▼

98. The Mil Mi-6 'Hook', seen here in company with an ASU-57 airborne assault gun in the foreground, represented a big step in Soviet helicopter development when it first flew in 1957. Large clamshell doors in the rear enable it to lift wheeled or tracked vehicles, such as the ASU-57, up to a limit of some 26,450lb. This photograph was taken during Exercise 'Dnieper' in 1967. (Novosti)

99. Soviet Border Guards race to a Mil Mi-8 'Hip-E' during a 'practice alert'. The nose-mounted 12.7mm machine-gun is visible, as are the stores pylons with provision for three rocket pods and two AT-2 'Swatter' anti-tank guided weapons on either side of the aircraft. (N. Zhiganov/Tass)

100. Derived from the Mi-6 'Hook', the Mil Mi-10 'Harke' was developed as a flying crane in the early 1960s. It is capable of carrying a 33,070lb payload on a platform beneath its fuselage. Although several 'Harkes' are in military service, it was used mainly in the civil role. (Tass)

101. A more recent development, this time from the Mi-8 'Hip' series, is the boat-hulled Mil Mi-14 'Haze' shore-based anti-submarine helicopter. Similar to the Sea King, it has rear-mounted stabilizing sponsons, a MAD array and an under-fuselage search radar in the nose.

102. Another Mi-8 'Hip' version was shown for the first time at the Paris Air Show in 1981. Designated Mil Mi-17, this helicopter will undoubtedly replace earlier versions of the 'Hip' in Soviet and Warsaw Pact military service. Note the shortened engine nacelles and the lengthened fuel sponsons with an air intake on the port sponson, presumably for an integral auxiliary power unit. (MJG)

100▲

101▲ 102▼

▲103

103. When the Soviets took to designing a gunship helicopter, they actually produced a dual-role gunship/assault helicopter, designated the Mil Mi-24 'Hind'. This photograph shows the initial 'Hind-A' version, which was first deployed in Eastern Europe in 1974. Note the stub wings with four UB-32 rocket pods and four AT-2 Swatter anti-tank guided missiles. In addition to a flight crew of four, the 'Hind-A' had provision for a squad of eight fully-equipped troops. A 12.7mm machine-gun is carried in an under-nose turret. (via UK MoD)

104. The latest product of the Mil design bureau in the Soviet Union is the Mi-26 'Halo', which is designed to replace the Mi-6 and Mi-10. 'Halo' made its public debut in the West at the 1981 Paris Air Show, where this photograph was taken. Despite its Aeroflot markings, 'Halo' undoubtedly will have a military career. (MJG)

105. The 'Hind-D' is another, more recent version of the Mi-24. The forward fuselage has been redesigned to carry the pilot and co-pilot/gunner in a tandem configuration, similar to the AH-1/AH-64 series. Note the four rocket pods and launch rails for AT-2 'Swatter' anti-tank guided missiles, plus the under-nose 12.7mm machine-gun, slaved to a sensor pack also mounted beneath the nose. This version has been used by Soviet forces in Afghanistan. (via US MoD)

106. The 'Hind-D' version of the Mi-24 has been further developed to carry AT-6 'Spiral' anti-tank guided missiles in place of 'Swatters'. This head-on view clearly shows the two sensor packages either side of the nose, with the 12.7mm machine-gun between the two. It also shows the port-mounted tail rotor (compare with 'Hind-A', which has it mounted on the starboard side of the tail) and the air intake deflector plates, which in this view appear to blank off the air intakes. (via US DoD)

▼104

◄107

108▲

109▲ 110▼

107. The Sikorsky S-61 design has been a successful helicopter since its first flight in 1959. Apart from being progressively improved and adapted for many roles, it has been manufactured under licence in Italy, Japan and the UK. This photograph shows the ultimate US Navy ASW version of the S-61, the SH-3H Sea King. Converted from the SH-3G, it offers a multi-mission capability for ASW and fleet missile defence. The SH-3H is equipped with advanced dunking sonar (illustrated), active and passive sonobuoys, MAD gear and electronic support measures (ESM). A total of some 163 SH-3Hs were built. (Sikorsky Aircraft)

108. The CH-3C transport variant is another derivative of the S-61, seen here taking on fuel from a US Navy KC-130 Hercules. The CH-3C incorporated many design changes, the most obvious of which was a new rear boom to allow a loading ramp to be installed in the rear fuselage. In all, 41 CH-3Cs were built for the USAF, followed by 42 improved CH-3E models. However, it was in its air rescue role (especially over Vietnam) that the HH-3E became famous as the 'Jolly Green Giant', picking up aircrews

shot down over friendly and hostile territory. (Sikorsky Aircraft)

109. Sikorsky's S-65A design became the CH-53A Sea Stallion in service with the US Navy. A step upwards from the CH-3 series, it was adapted as a heavy lift helicopter for the US Marine Corps. Later, the US Navy adapted the type as a heli-borne mine countermeasures system, receiving 30 under the designation RH-53D. Iran was also supplied with six RH-53Ds, and it is ironic to record that the ill-fated attempt to rescue the Tehran hostages was mounted using modified RH-53Ds. (Sikorsky Aircraft)

110. The USAF saw in the Sea Stallion a replacement for their HH-3Es in the air rescue role, and ordered 72 in both HH-53C and -E configurations in the late 1960s. The USAF are currently modifying to HH-53H configuration a number of the 'Super Jolly Green Giants', as they became known, under a programme called Pave Low III, with FLIR, terrain-avoidance radar and inertial navigation. This photograph shows one of the HH-53Cs of the 67th Aerospace Rescue and Recovery Squadron of the USAF, based at Woodbridge in the UK, prior to its Pave Low III conversion. (USAF Europe)

▲111

▲112 ▼113   114▶

111. The CH-53D is the current heavy assault helicopter serving with the US Marine Corps. Powered by two T64-GE-413 turboshaft engines, the CH-53D is capable of lifting 55 combat-ready marines. This helicopter is from HMH-461, which is based on the USS *Saipan*. (MJG)

112. One of the 112 Sikorsky CH-53G medium lift helicopters of the West German Army, most of which were built under licence by VFW-Fokker in West Germany. (MJG)

113. In 1973, the CH-53 was chosen for further development with three engines as the future heavy-lift multi-purpose

helicopter of the US Navy and Marine Corps. This photograph of one of the first of the CH-53E version (as the type was designated) shows that the third T64-GE-415 turboshaft engine has been placed on the port side of the fuselage top.

114. Having lost a high proportion of its RH-53D fleet on the Tehran raid, and needing a new mine countermeasures helicopter for the 1990s, the US Navy is procuring a number of MH-53E Super Stallions for this role. This head-on view of the first MH-53 clearly shows the three engine intakes, as well as the tailboom canted over to port, and the starboard stabilizer. (Sikorsky Aircraft)

▲115

115. The CH-54 Tarhe (alias the S-64 Skycrane in civil guise) came earlier in the development chain than the CH-53 but is used by the US Army in small numbers as, literally, a sky crane for moving heavy, bulky loads. This photograph shows a CH-54 moving a fire unit of the US Roland mobile SAM system. (Sikorsky Aircraft)

116. The Sikorsky S-69 Advancing Blade Concept demonstrator, designated XH-59A, which has been used for this task since 1974. Briefly, this concept entails the use of two coaxial contra-rotating rigid rotors designed to take advantage of the aerodynamic lift potential of the advancing blade. The retreating blades are 'unloaded' of lift at high speeds with the advancing blades taking the bulk of the lift. This removes the penalties of retreating blade stall and also the need for a supplementary wing to add speed and agility to a helicopter. (Sikorsky Aircraft)

117. The major programme presently underway at Sikorsky Aircraft is the S-70 Utility Tactical Transport Aircraft System (UTTAS), now designated the UH-60A Black Hawk. This model was selected as the winner of the UTTAS contest in 1976, after a fly-off with the Boeing Vertol YUH-61A. Able to carry eleven fully-equipped troops plus a crew of three, the Black Hawk can also carry a useful 8,000lb underslung cargo load as an alternative. (Sikorsky Aircraft)

118. Sikorsky has recently offered a further development of the UH-60A Black Hawk in the shape of an External Stores Support System (ESSS). Basically an external pylon system, it offers the capability to fit the UH-60A with offensive stores or external fuel tanks or even cargo. (Sikorsky Aircraft)

119. Another version of the Black Hawk currently under evaluation is this EH-60A 'Quick Fix' special electronics mission aircraft. Its role is to intercept, monitor and jam enemy radio communications. Another special variant, the EH-60B SOTAS (Stand-Off Target Acquisition System) fitted with a rotating underbelly antenna, is currently 'on ice' while the radar system is being developed. (Sikorsky Aircraft)

▲116 ▼117

◀**120**

121▲

120, 121. Mention has already been made of the LAMPS programme in the US Navy. These illustrations show the SH-60B Sea Hawk air vehicle for the LAMPS III programme. Based on the engine/airframe of the UH-60A Black Hawk, it is being fitted with a new avionics suite to equip it for the ASW and anti-ship surveillance and targeting (ASST) roles. It is interesting to note that the LAMPS III contract was placed with the avionics systems contractor, IBM, and Sikorsky's role is that of major sub-contractor supplying the air vehicle – a further example of the advance of modern technology. One of the prototype SH-60B Sea Hawk helicopters (**120**) is shown preparing to land on the USS *McInerney* during sea trials. The trial lasted 170 days and the aircraft completed 600 flight hours. Note the homing torpedoes, MAD gear and large underbelly radome for the search radar. (Sikorsky Aircraft)

122. The latest military helicopter from the Sikorsky stable is the Utility variant of their S-76 Mk.II civil helicopter. This photograph shows the company demonstrator fitted with weapons pylons mounting unguided rocket pods during a weapons trial programme, which also confirmed the type's suitability as a weapons platform. Sikorsky are also offering this version with a Pratt and Whitney Canada PT6B-36 power plant as an alternative to the usual Allison 250-C30 turboshaft engines. (Sikorsky Aircraft)

122▼

▲123

123. The first major successful helicopter built in the UK after the early Dragonfly, Widgeon and Sycamore, was the Westland Whirlwind, the Sikorsky S-55 built under licence. This Whirlwind HAR.2, powered by the early Pratt and Whitney R-1340-40 piston engine, is about to release a case of mines for the mechanical minelaying train below. The aircraft was part of 225 Sqn., RAF, and was later fitted with the Gnome H.1000 turboshaft engine being re-designated HAR.10. (MJG)

124. With its distinctive all-yellow finish, the Whirlwind was for many years a familiar sight in its search and rescue role around Britain's coastline. The last Whirlwind SAR helicopters have only recently been retired in favour of the Wessex and Sea King.

▼124

125. The Sikorsky S-58 followed the S-55 on Westland's production lines as the Wessex. Early versions were fitted with a single Napier Gazelle turboshaft, as illustrated by this SAR Wessex HAR.1 of 771 Sqn., based at Portland in 1975. Note that in this shot the winchman is also equipped as a diver. (HMS *Ospr*

126. The next mark of Wessex to enter Royal Navy service was the improved HAS.3 anti-submarine version with search radar and dunking sonar. These helicopters are part of 737 Sqn., which acts as both training unit and headquarters unit for the helicopters deployed with County-class guided missile destroyers. The Wessex HAS.3 was basically an improved HAS.1, employing the same airframe and engine. (HMS *Osprey*)

▲127 ▼128

127. The Wessex was also selected for RAF service as the HC.2, but for this mark the Gazelle engine was replaced by a pair of Gnomes coupled to the single-drive shaft. This photograph shows a 28 Sqn. Wessex HC.2 exercising with the Royal Hong Kong Police. (JSPRS, Hong Kong)

128. The naval counterpart of the RAF HC.2 was the Wessex HU.5, again with twin Gnome engines. It serves in the commando assault role, and during the Falklands conflict proved a valuable asset to the Task Force. (MJG)

129. Initially developed as the Saunders-Roe P.531, this helicopter became the basis for both a naval ASW helicopter, suitable for small-ship operations, and an Army utility helicopter. The P.531 became first the Wasp and then the Scout. This photograph shows a Wasp HAS.1 configured for anti-ship operations firing an AS.12 anti-ship missile. (HMS *Osprey*)

130. With the introduction of the Lynx into Royal Navy service, earlier Wasps have become available for re-export as required. This photograph shows one of four Wasps that were refurbished by Westlands and delivered to the Indonesian Navy in 1981. (Westland Helicopters)

131. As the wheel-equipped Wasp was developed for the Royal Navy, so the Scout was developed for the Army Air Corps. This example shows a Scout AH.1 configured with four SS.11 anti-tank wire-guided missiles, a roof-mounted sight and bulged rear doors (to accommodate a stretcher internally). (MJG)

129▲

130▲ 131▼

▲132

▲133 ▼134

132. The inclusion of the ubiquitous Bell 47 Sioux in this section of the book may at first seem curious. However, despite the design stretching back to 1947, Westlands built a number of Sioux under licence from Agusta of Italy, who in turn were Bell licencees during the mid-1960s. Designated Model 47G-3B-4, the Sioux AH.1 was a popular light observation helicopter in Army service. This photograph shows a Sioux of the Air Platoon, Royal Tank Regiment, making a rendezvous with a Ferret scout car in Eastern Arabia in 1968. (British Official)

133. The RAF's first twin rotor helicopter was the Bristol/Westland Belvedere. Initially derived from the Bristol 173 passenger helicopter, the type was refined as the Bristol 192 for RAF service. During further refinement, Bristol Helicopters were absorbed into Westland Helicopters, and the 192 became the Belvedere HC.1. This photograph shows a Belvedere of 66 Sqn. in the Far East during the Malaysian confrontation. (John Birch)

134. After the Wessex, the next Sikorsky-designed project to be developed by Westland was the S-61 in its SH-3D form. This became, initially, the Sea King HAS.1 for ASW duties with the Royal Navy. Powered by a pair of Gnome H.1400 turboshafts it proved an effective helicopter, not only in the ASW role but also in the SAR role. One of the first export customers for the Westland Sea King was West Germany, which took 22 of the SAR Mk.41 version, one of which is illustrated here. Note the five-blade tail rotor, which was later changed to a six-blade one. (Westland Helicopters)

135. The improved ASW variant of the Sea King, the HAS.2 (with six-blade tail rotor) embarked on HMS *Ark Royal* for her final commission in April 1979. Note the folded main rotor blades for ease of stowage below decks. (MJG)

136. The RAF had long cherished the hope that the Sea King would be a Whirlwind SAR replacement. They were able finally to procure the type in the late 1970s, with first deliveries of the Sea King HAR.3 being made in 1979. (Westland Helicopters)

▲137

137. The most recent ASW version of the Sea King, the HAS.5, which has a larger dorsal radome to house the Sea Searcher radar. This photograph shows an 826 Sqn. helicopter on the deck of HMS *Hermes* during her voyage to the South Atlantic. Note the AN/ASQ-81(V)-2 MAD equipment on the trailing edge of the undercarriage sponson, which is similar to the installation on the US Navy's SH-3H Sea King. Although this photograph is an official release, the UK MoD declined to comment on the MAD installation. (CINC Fleet)

138. Two examples of the very latest version of the Sea King on their delivery flight to HMS *Illustrious*. Based on the HAS.2 engine/airframe, two Sea Kings were hastily adapted to carry the Searchwater radar of the RAF's Nimrod MR.2 maritime patrol and ASW aircraft, to fill the airborne early warning gap made patently obvious during the Falklands conflict. These two conversions were made and test-flown in the remarkably short time of eleven weeks, and are now deployed on board HMS *Illustrious*. Further conversions (three to five Sea Kings)

138▲ 139▼

are expected in the future. (Westland Helicopters)

139. Two of the Commando Mk.2s sold to Egypt were configured for VIP use. This photograph shows one of these aircraft at Yeovil, prior to delivery. (MJG)

140. The Royal Navy were slow to latch on to Commando development, and it was only after the 105mm Light Gun was adopted by the Commando Battery of the Royal Artillery that attention was paid to the type. As the Light Gun could not be carried as an underslung load beneath the Wessex HU.5, Sea Kings had to be employed to lift them from ship to shore, thus detracting from their prime ASW role. A decision to order a batch of Commandos, but with folding rotor blades, was made in the late-1970s to support the Royal Marines and their artillery component. To maintain the Sea King genealogy, the designation Sea King HC.4 was adopted for the fifteen helicopters ordered. This photograph shows an aircraft of 846 Sqn. at Yeovilton, after its return from the Falklands conflict. (MJG)

140▼

141. The naval variant of the WG.13, the Lynx HAS.2 of the Royal Navy (airborne), which is shown here with the Dutch SAR variant, the UH-14A Lynx (on the ground). The Royal Netherlands Navy has also received an ASW version of the Lynx in two marks: the UH-14B (Lynx Mk.27), which is generally similar to the British HAS.2, but with Alcatel dunking sonar as fitted to the French naval Lynx; and the UH-14C, which is fitted with MAD gear. (P/O L. R. Warr)

142. The final third of the Anglo-French helicopter package was the WG.13 design, led by Westlands, which became the Lynx. As with the P.531, the WG.13 was developed in both Army and Navy variants. This photograph shows the Army Lynx AH.1, fully equipped for the anti-tank role with eight TOW missiles and a roof-mounted sight. (MJG)

143. This photograph of a Royal Navy Lynx HAS.2 is interesting in that the aircraft is camouflaged in an Army pattern. In the absence of official comment, one can only speculate that it has been used for special operations of some description. (MJG)

144. In addition to its ASW role, the Lynx HAS.2 can be fitted with BAeD Sea Skua anti-ship missiles. This photograph shows a Sea Skua-equipped Lynx serving with the British Task Force in the South Atlantic. The Sea Skua was used with great success during the Falklands conflict. (Royal Navy)

142▲

◄141

143▲ 144▼

▲145

▲146 ▼147

145. Westlands have developed the Lynx further to produce a utility helicopter, designated Westland 30, for both civil and military applications. This photograph shows the Westland 30 in military guise, embarking an anti-tank missile team. (Westland Helicopters)

146. Taking the Army Lynx programme one step further, Westlands have proposed a future third generation helicopter, known as Lynx 3, with increased capability and survivability. Note the eight Hellfire anti-tank missiles, four Stinger self-defence missiles, new blade-tip profile and both mast- and nose-mounted sighting equipment. (Westland Helicopters)

147. The latest advance in the cooperative field is the Anglo-Italian EH-101 Sea King Replacement helicopter. Agusta of Italy and Westland Helicopters of the UK have formed a joint company, European Helicopter Industries, to develop the EH-101, which will be available in the late 1980s to replace existing Royal Navy Sea Kings and Italian Navy SH-3Ds. This photograph shows the latest configuration of the helicopter with the Ferranti Blue Kestrel radar under the nose. The EH-101 will be used for both ASW and ASST roles and will be able to operate from the new Type 23 frigates under development for the Royal Navy, as well as larger vessels. (Westland Helicopters)